Never Alarm a

Poems and drawings for kids

by
Steve Attewell

www.laughedmysocksoff.com

1st edition published 2021

First published in 2021

All contents copyright © 2021 by Steve Attewell. All rights reserved. No part of this document may be reproduced or transmitted in any form, by any means (electronic, photocopying, recording, or otherwise) without the prior written permission of the publisher.

Any trademarks, service marks, product names or named features are assumed to be the property of their respective owners, and are used only for reference. There is no implied endorsement by the use of these terms.

Copyright © 2021 Steve Attewell

All rights reserved.

ISBN: 9798728912231

Imprint: Independently published

At school I was told off for drawing in my books.

The poems that are in this book

1	Never alarm a llama
2	A, bee, see
3	Cat flap
5	Eleven melons and a lemon
6	Flute Badger
9	I drew a door upon a wall
12	I thought I thunk a think
14	Itchy
15	Lost
18	Stupid fly
20	The bounce I did
22	The invisible hamster
25	The longest poem ever written
26	Things I don't like
28	This is not a poem
30	Tim the caterpillar
34	Upside down
35	What book to read tonight?
36	What's a rhyme?
37	Words
38	Yesssss

Never alarm a llama

Never alarm a llama,
Don't perturb a bird,
Never scare a squirrel,
Or make a dog disturbed,

Never poke a penguin,
Or badger a badger or bear,
Don't impede a centipede,
Or give a squid a scare,

Or stare at stoats,
Or tickle goats,
Or bat a cat,
Or throw a crow,
Or flick a gnat,
Or goad a toad,

'Cos that's not very fair.

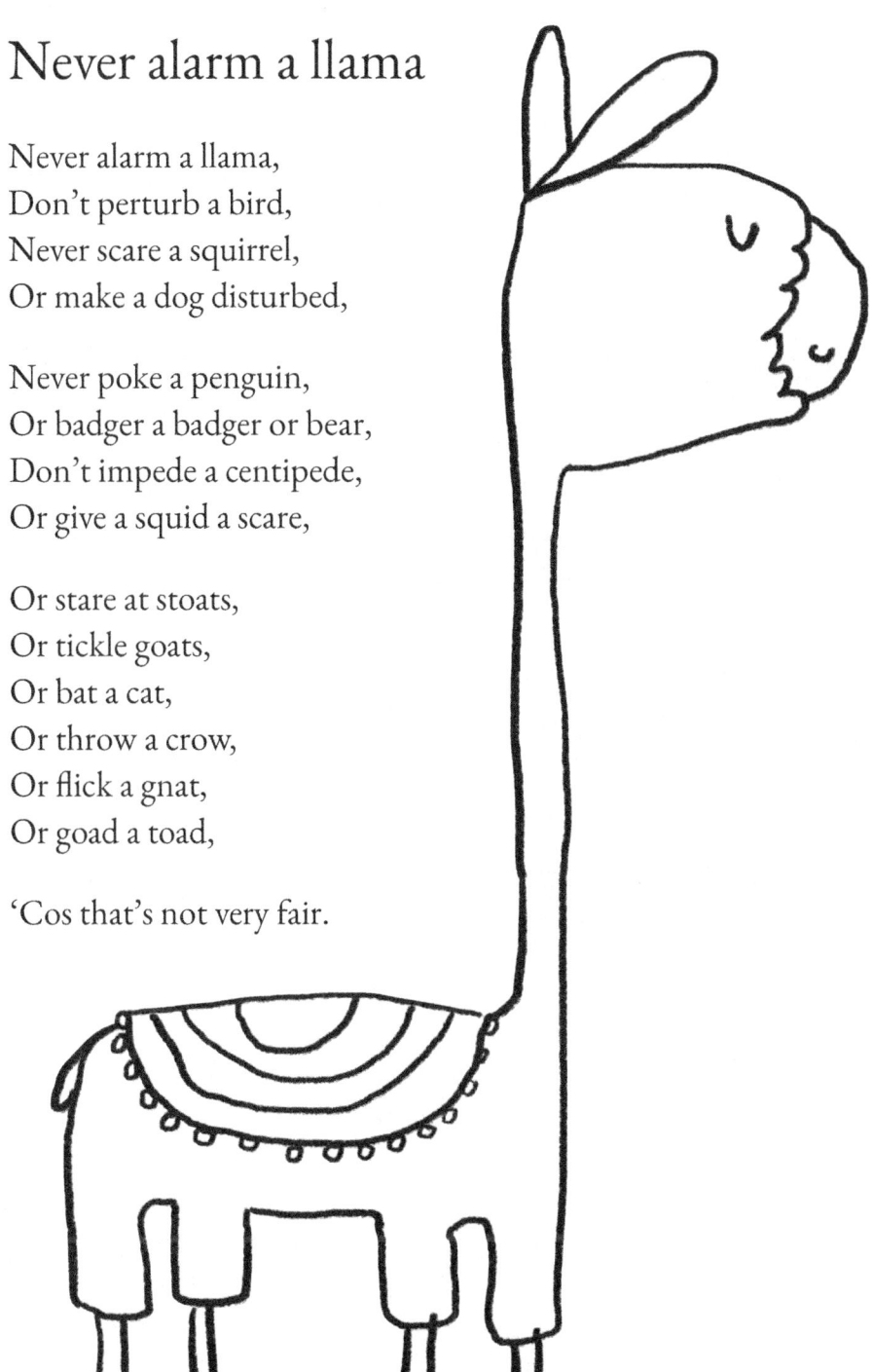

A, bee, see

A, bee, see,
That bee's been seen,

I see you bee,

When young, my mum got stung on her tongue,
And a numb tongue's no fun,

So I don't want you to bee here,
I think you should bee somewhere else.

Cat flap

There's a cat tapping at that cat flap...

It is my flap,
But not my cat,

I left the cat flap locked to stop,
That cat from coming in,

It comes at night (though uninvited),
To push and scratch,
And bash that hatch,

I think it knows I left a pair,
Of fish bones in the bin,

It's getting in a flap that cat,

Tapping,

Pushing,

Scratching,

Bashing at that flap,

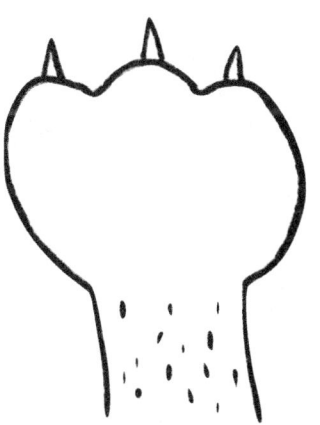

Now my cat flap's snapped.

It's in.

It's jumped into the bin.

Eating bits of fish therein.

"Drat!"

That   *pushing*,
Heeeeeeaaaaaving,
T a p p i n g,
Scrrrrrat-ching,
BASHING,
Cat - flap - *snap*ping cat.

Eleven melons and a lemon

A single dangly bell's lingering dingle,

Whose two tiny shiny shoes are these please?

Three bees buzzing lazily in trees,

Four clawed paws clacking on a cracked floor,

Five fancy fish flipping chips into a skip,

Six thick bricks settled on some sticks,

Seven thieving venomous snakes named Steven,

I hate that these eight crates of juicy dates came late,

A sublime line of nine fine limes,

When will Ben give back my ten black pens again?

Eleven melons and a lemon.

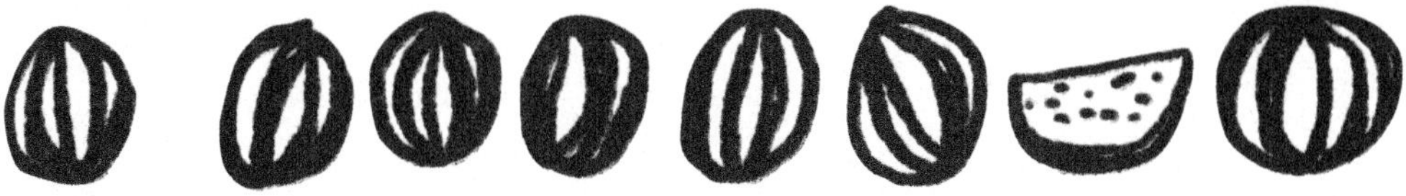

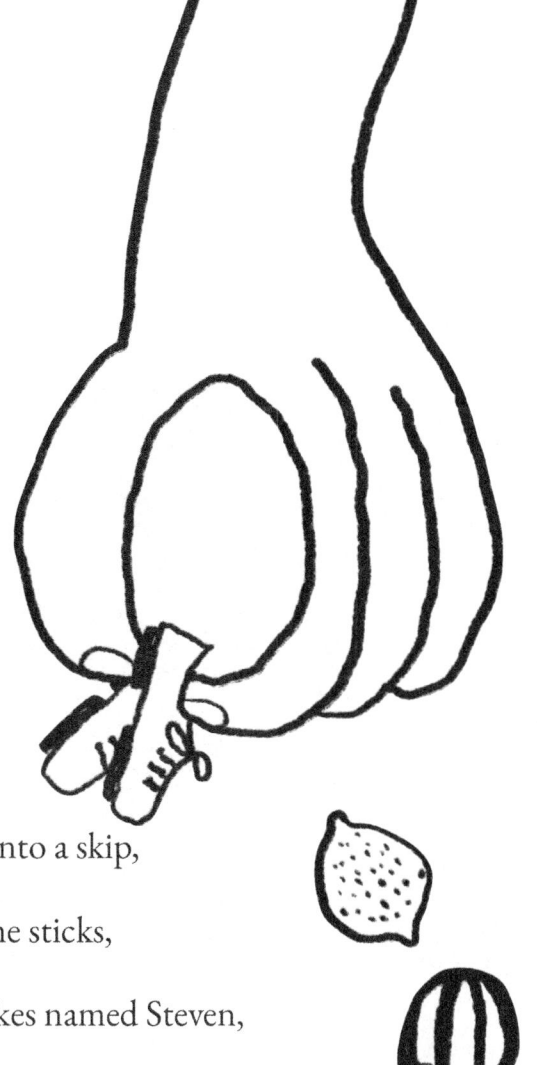

Flute Badger

Flute badger, Flute badger, play us a tune,
Flute badger blow like you blow a balloon,

Huff and then puff, so your cheeks turn to red,
Jiggle and jive in your flute badger shed,

Play your jazz-flute for the creatures around;
All of them dance to your badger jazz sound,

Foxes come, kicking back, snapping their fingers,
At flute badger's happenin' sound as it lingers...

Echoing through all the trees in the wood,
Rocking the night like those badger beats should,

Squirrels a-tippetty-tap on their logs,
Earwigs click jiggling twigs and the frogs...

Leap and croak loudly in time with the beat,
Pigs dance a jig on their shufflin' feet,

Fireflies flash and they light up the night,
Hedgehogs do backflips, a wondrous sight,

Otters are shaking, they rattle and roll,
Rats dance with cats and the vipers and voles,

There's banging and bumping and booming and more,
Rabbits are thumping their feet on the floor,

Critters and creatures are playing their song,
Those that aren't playing are clapping along,

Flute badger, flute badger, play us a tune,
Jazz-flute's our excuse to dance under the moon.

I drew a door upon a wall

I drew a door upon a wall,
To hide behind with fearful mind,
And knocked upon it; knock, knock, knock,
Expecting no reply,

I strained my ears and listened hard,
And then I heard, I did, I swear,
Shuffled feet, a mumble, then,
A voice say, "WHO IS THERE?"

Startled, stepping back, wide-eyed,
I looked upon my simple scrawl,
And wondered who could be behind,
My drawing on the wall,

I knocked again, a single rap,
A tap, upon the door I drew,
And then I heard, as clear as day,
A voice say, "WHO ARE YOU?"

I whispered then, "I'm just a boy,
Who drew a door, through which to hide,
I did not think to hear a voice,
Upon the other side."

"Are you sure you wish to be,
Behind the door, this side, with me?"
The voice replied as if to guide,
My mind to then agree,

"Is your desire to sit and stay,
Still in the place you know to be,
A fearful place indeed, or see,
What lies this side with me?"

"A warning, though, I give to you,
That once you open up this door,
Escaping from your strife, you'll stay,
This side forever more."

"Do you choose to face your fate,
Stay on your side, or will you hide,
And choose to leave that life behind,
To let me be your guide?"

I thought of what had scarred me so,
Making farewell thoughts take shape,
Moving me to draw this door,
To give me an escape,

Then, a change of heart progressed,
Unspoiled thoughts fought to the fore,
The love of those that know my soul,
Leave that forever more?

The hearts and minds of artists beat,
Against that tide of churlish ways,
And rose me, then, upon my feet,
To act upon the day,

Resolve struck soundly in my chest,
To halt my dusk, my evenfall,
Against the door I took my cloth,
And washed it from the wall.

I thought I thunk a think

I thunk a thought but now it's gone,
I'm writing this instead,

It came to me from nowhere, but,
I lost it in my head,

I looked behind the sofa,
To see if it was there,

But all I found were fluffy chunks,
No thoughts beneath the chair,

I turned my eyes a-right around,
Backwards, to my brains,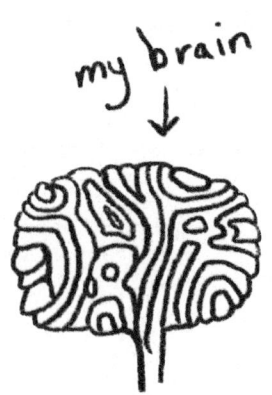

I thought I saw a think go past,
Around my mind again,

But all it was was nothing,
No think or thunk or thought,

No ideas are here today...

Itchy

An itch I have,
An itchy head,
An itch I'll spread,

An itch you have,
Now I've said,
About my head,

An itch I put,
From on my head,
Into a book,

An itch that moves,
Out of a book,
And into you,

My itch is gone,
Now it's with you.

Phew!

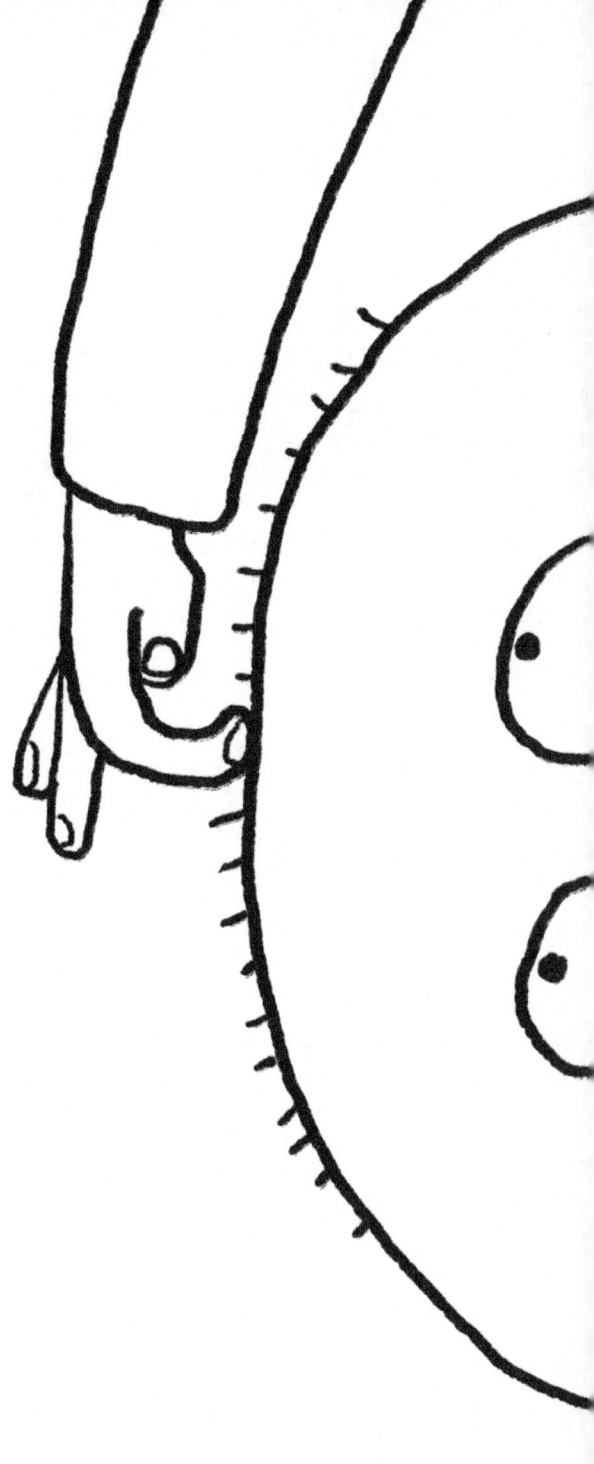

Lost

I'm sure I had it yesterday,
But now it's lost alright,
It's one of those things with pictures in,
That switches off at night,

You know.
Those things.
That come and go.
They're sometimes fast,
They're sometimes slow,
The morning's better, 'cos they're fresher,
They go all fuzzy under pressure,

Oh yes,
Of course,
It came to me,

So simple,
Elementary,

I found it,
'Twas my memory.

It's drak inhere

It's drak inhere,
too drack to see;
Tpp drark to wrute a powem,

But I got teh itch,
Teh writnig bug.

and poemds. arw a flownig,

\

I wizh I haf a tprch in here/
a cnadle ore a ligjt;'
Or smoething to ignight.
or it waz day adn npt teh nifght/

As evven thoigh a powem"s flownin;
I;m shpwing thst it,s fqr tpp drack/
Tpo drack to wryte a powme/

Stupid fly

As I write this poem,
A fly will not stop goin',
Around and 'round my head,
I tend to lose my thread,
About my poem,
'Cos it's goin',
'Round my head,
It won't stop flying,
'Round my head,

My head,

I said:

"Stop your flying 'round my head,
While I am going 'bout my poem."

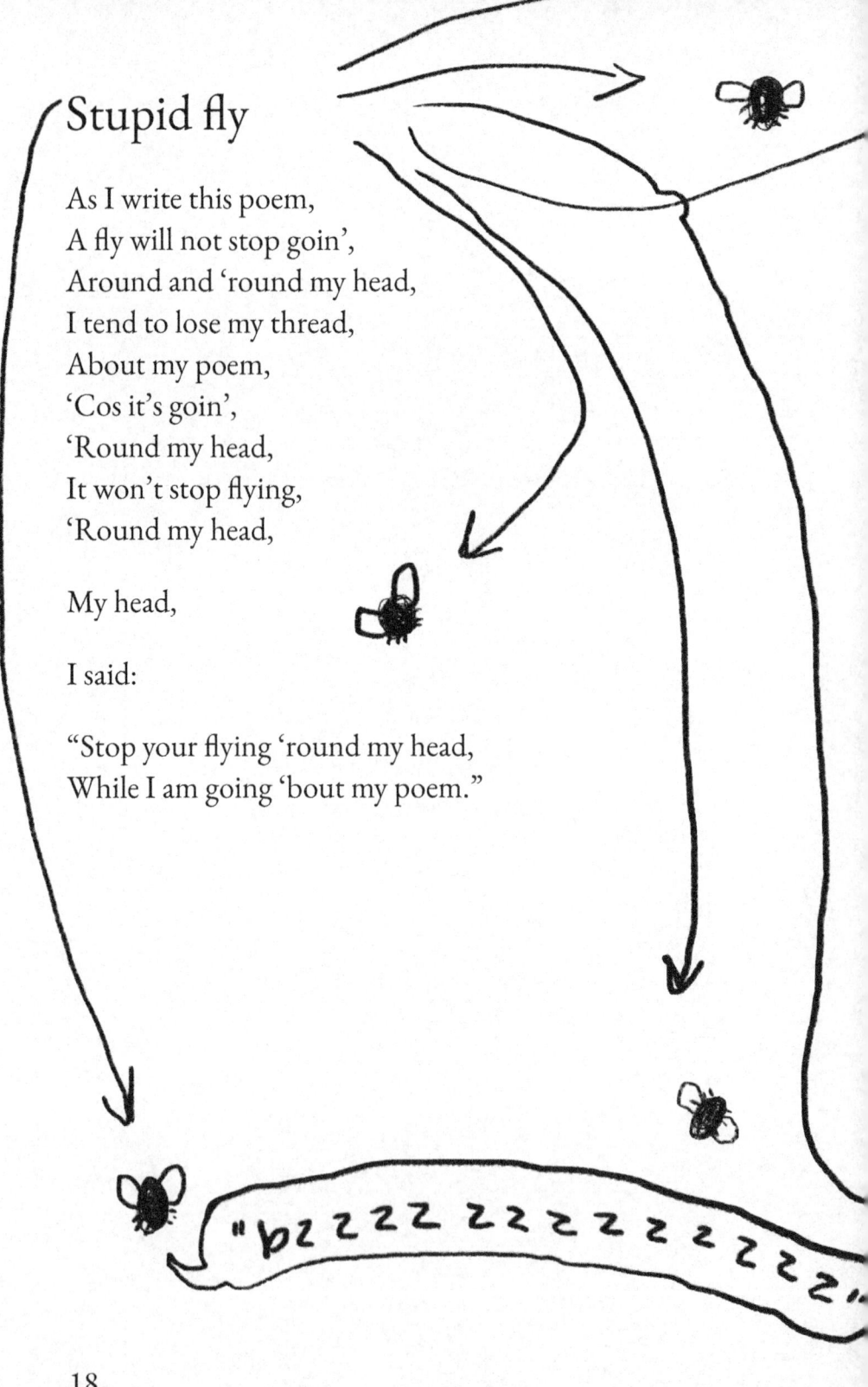

Now it's stopped,
But where's it gone?
I'm pretty sure it won't be long,
Before the buzzing starts once more,
As it launches from the floor,
Why will it not fly out the door?
Instead it thuds against the glass,
The silly thing - it won't get past!

It's headed for my head again,
Around and 'round my head again,
Right near my ear and back again,
And so I've lost my track again,
I'll never concentrate again,
I'll never write a rhyme again,
My verses will be worse again…

I'll not complete this poem,
The way that this is goin'.

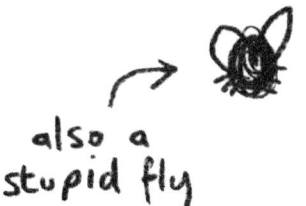

The bounce I did

The bounce I did was big,
The bounce I did was high,
The bounce I did was my last bid,
At hanging on the sky,

The slide I did went whoosh,
The slide I did went weeeee!
The slide I did was the biggest skid,
You'll ever, ever see,

The doink I did was tiny,
The doink I did was small,
The doink I did to that other kid,
Was hardly there at all,

The smile I did was broad,
The smile I did was wide,
It stretched across from my left cheek,
Right to the other side,

The jump I did was huge,
The jump I did was long,
I skipped and hopped and jumped all day,
And sang a little song.

The invisible hamster

My hamster is invisible,
He's there for all to see,
Except that he's not there at all,
Where could my hamster be?

Last night I left him in his cage,
He snuggled down and snored,
But 'though his cage is closed and locked,
He's not there anymore,

He would have packed his suitcase,
If going on vacation,
He must now be invisible,
It's the only explanation,

I told my friends about my pet,
They came along to view,
The hamster that could not be seen,
And soon there was a queue,

That stretched across the landing,
Down the stairs, and out the door,
They want to see a hamster that's,
Not even there at all,

A writer for the paper came,
And, staring at the cage,
Wrote the story, there it was,
Upon next day's front page,

The mayor came up to my room,
On 21st of May,
And said, "I do declare that this,
Is Invisible Hamster Day."

The phone was ringing off the hook,
So many came to see,
We sold refreshments on the lawn,
But mum ran out of tea,

The queue was getting longer now,
A crowd appeared next day,
Dad said, "They'll wear the carpet out,
We'll have to make them pay!"

Police turned up, the army came,
A General said to me,
"How is it that your hamster has,
Invisibility?"

I thought quite hard on this and said,
"It's really pretty weird,
One moment he was there and then,
He just plain disappeared!"

The General said "We'll take your pet,
And do a lot of tests,
And poke it with a pointy stick,
I think it's for the best."

They took the cage away,
I'll never see him anymore...
Then to my surprise,
I found my hamster on the floor.

The longest poem ever written

The longest poem ever written,
Wasn't this 'un.

if you can think of a poem that only has two lines you can write it below ↓

Things I don't like

1. Long lists

2. Wasted space

Please write a poem or draw a picture or something on this page so that the space is not wasted. Thank you.

(If you can't think of anything to put here, you could draw a picture of yourself drawing a picture of a cat. Then ask a friend to draw a picture of you doing that)

This is not a poem

This is not a poem. It hardly even rhymes. I've split it up by sentences. Instead of separate lines.

Sometimes I've changed the rhythm so that it doesn't trip off the tongue which you might find annoying.

When I was at school I had a teacher who

1) loved rules and

2) was very, very rude.

If I was still at school and that teacher saw this poem they would say...

STEVEN! THIS IS NOT A POEM. NEVER EVER PUT THIS IN A POETRY BOOK. BECAUSE IT IS DEFINITELY NOT POETRY.

AND WHY HAVE YOU NOT USED QUOTATION MARKS AROUND THE BIT WHERE I SAY THIS?

But now look.

I've written a book.

And it's my book.

So i CAN bReAk aLL the RULez I want.

Tim the caterpillar

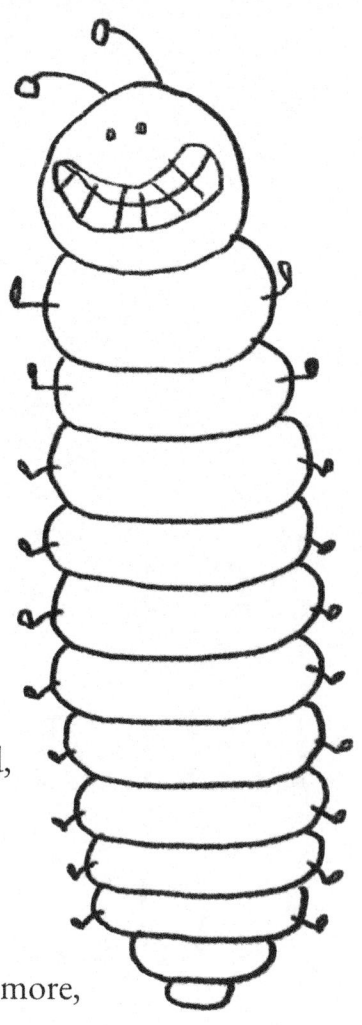

Tim the caterpillar wandered,
Round the wood one day,
Munching and a-crunching leaves,
And plants along the way,

"I cannot leave a leaf uneaten,"
Tim muttered as he searched,
The bottom of the oak and ash,
And top of silver birch,

His friends were at it too, you know,
They all were eating up,
The leaves and plants around the wood,
There's so much grub for grubs,

For days Tim ate. He could not think,
Of anything but food,
He thought, "I must munch more and more,
There's nothing else to do."

On day three our Tim felt tired,
As if he needed sleep,
Still he carried on and fed,
On leaf and leaf and leaf,

He looked around and realised then,
That all his friends had gone,

But Tim just kept on eating leaves,
On... and on... and on...

On the fourth day, after lunch,
Tim felt a funny feeling,
A little dizzy and perplexed,
It sent his tummy reeling,

But, Tim carried on with food,
To satisfy his hunger,
Until he felt so very tired,
He slipped into a slumber,

Fat and full, and satisfied,
(The cat that got the cream),
He lay and snored upon a branch,
And fell into a dream,

The spirit of the woodland came,
A white and whispy glow,
It called to him and said, "Now Tim,
There's something you should know,"

"You've eaten all that you can eat,
And, now that it is spring,
I need to tell you Tim, my lad,
You're bound for greater things,"

"You may have thought that life was great,
And eating's pretty clever,
But once you wake up from your sleep,
Your life will change forever."

When Tim woke he thought of what,
The woodland spirit said,
He yawned and tried to stretch himself,
But bumped his little head,

Befuddled, Timmy struggled,
He was squashed up in a ball,
Inside a case around him,
Now this won't do at all,

What's this, he thought,
He pushed and heaved until he saw a split,
Upon the wall and so he pulled,
And wiggled it a bit,

He pushed his head out through the hole,
And squeezed his body out,
He flopped, exhausted on a leaf,
And had a look about,

"My goodness, what are these," he cried,
Looking at the things,
That sat there flat, upon his back,
"They look a lot like wings,"

And then he saw he had six legs,
And feelers on his head,
He thought, "I never had all this,
Before I went to bed!"

From the corner of his eye,
He saw that something fluttered by,
The brightly coloured insect was,
A wondrous looking butterfly,

And then it slowly dawned on Tim,
To stretch and flap his new-found wings,
And lift into the sky above,
To find the joy that flight would bring,

Tim was happy as he flew,
And flapped and flitted, through the sky,
He and his friends would flutter by,
Now he was a butterfly.

Upside down

Did you turn the book around?
Or are you hanging upside down?

And if you are now upside down,
Did your smile turn to a frown?

If I made you so rotate,
And changed you from your happy state,
And gave to you a mood of worry,
I'm very, very, very sorry.

What book to read tonight?

A book transports the reader reading,
Line by line and lost in time,
To wondrous lands imagined in their,
Fixed and curious mind,

They give the chance to fall in love,
Or, trapped, betrayed, to crawl and hide,
In shadowy places clutching just,
A book to be your guide,

To laugh, to cry, to wonder why,
Those flights of fancy come to light,
They're free down at the library,
What book to read tonight?

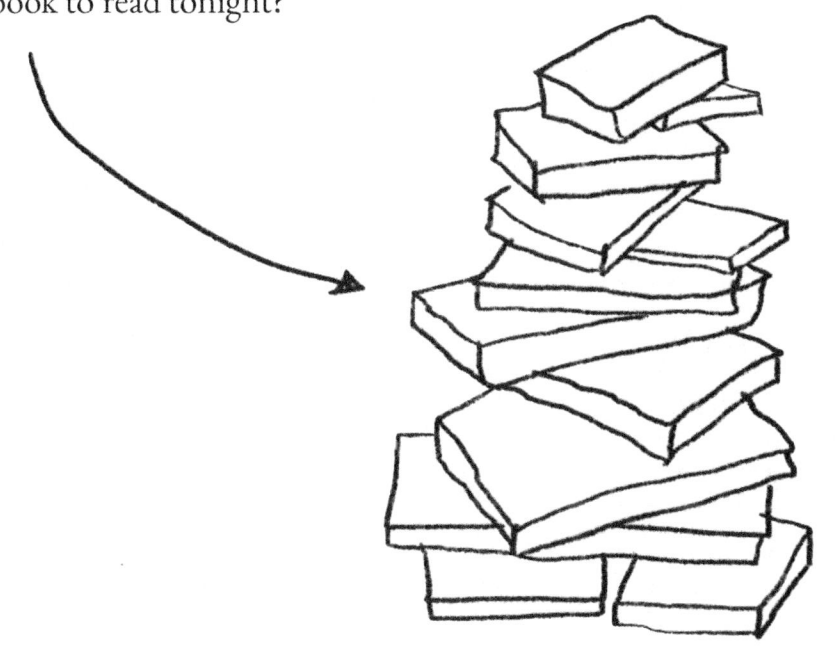

What's a rhyme?

What's a rhyme? Some fine lines?
Bouncing 'round your brain?

What's a poem? Is it showin',
Ends of words the same?

Is it given that a rhythm bounds along a line?

Is that what's going to take a poem,
From writing to a rhyme?

I mix these thinks and things around,
Never really knowin',

And see if, when I write them down,
I end up with a poem.

read this line all bouncy!

brain
same
fame
lame
game

poem
goin.
knowin.
flowin.
showin.

rhyme
time
fine
sublime
shine

Words

Word word word word,
Word word word,

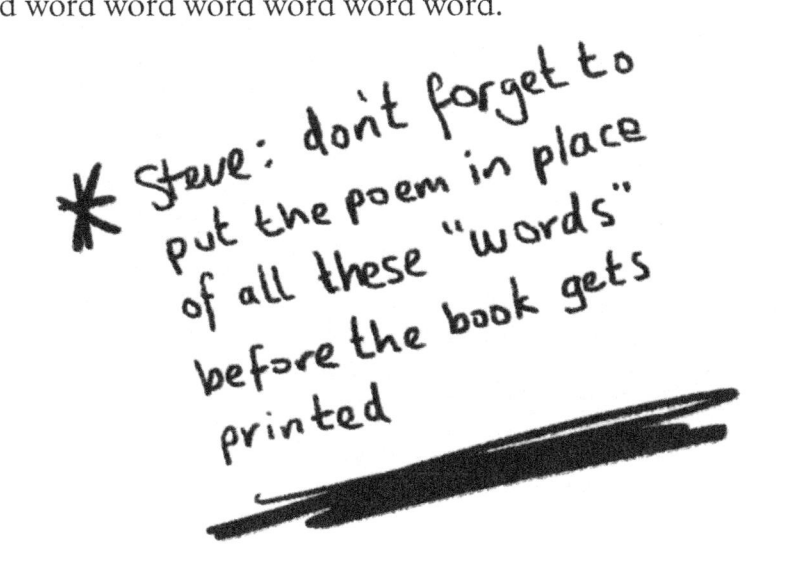

Word word word word,
Word word word,

Word word word,
Word word word,

Word word word word word word word.

※ Steve: don't forget to put the poem in place of all these "words" before the book gets printed

Yesssss

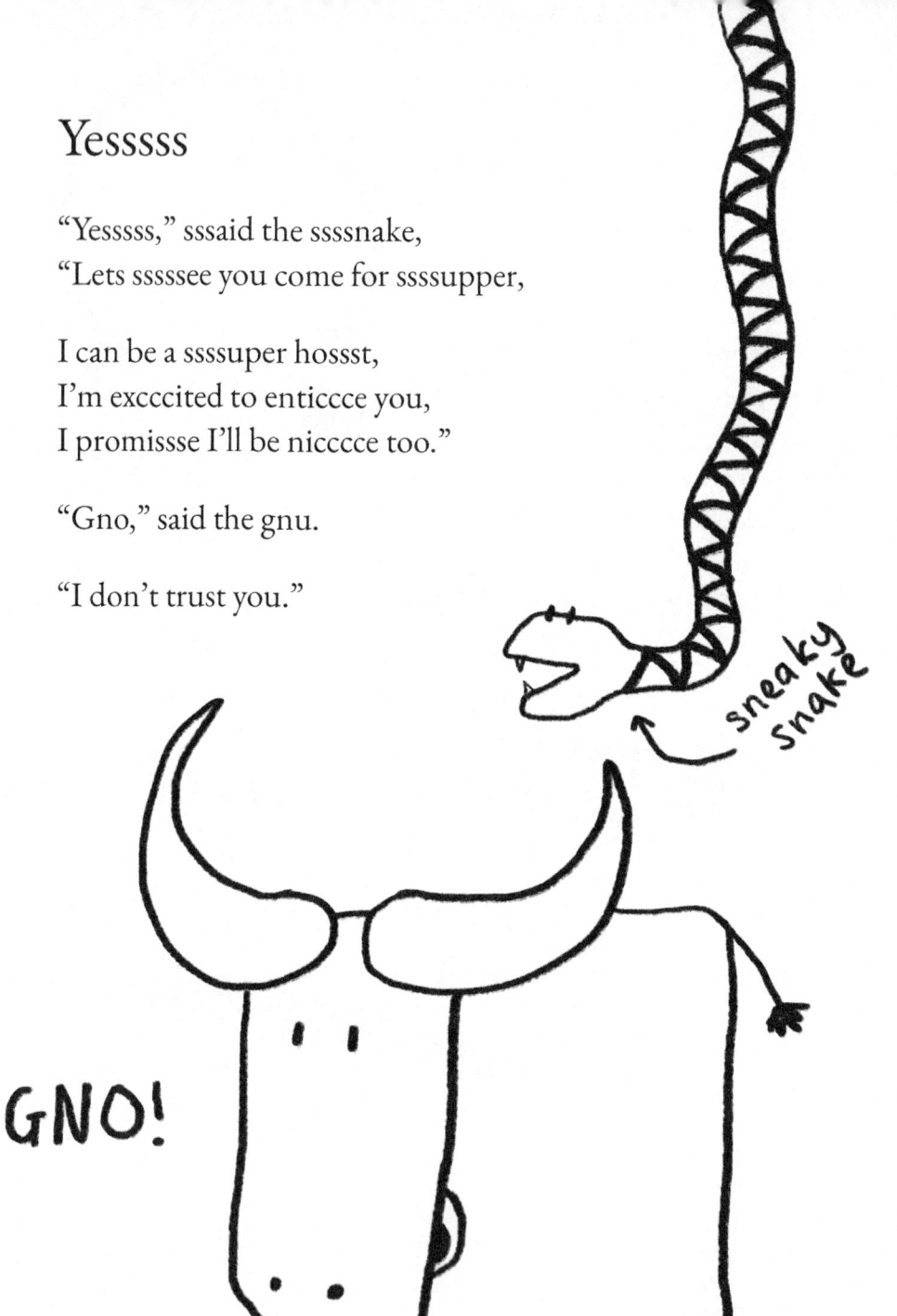

"Yesssss," sssaid the ssssnake,
"Lets sssssee you come for ssssupper,

I can be a ssssuper hossst,
I'm excccited to enticcce you,
I promissse I'll be nicccce too."

"Gno," said the gnu.

"I don't trust you."

another stupid fly
↓

So. That's it. I hope you liked these poems.

I also wrote some other books of poetry that you can find at my website laughedmysocksoff.com

There are some poetry videos on my website too.

I was told off for drawing silly pictures in my school books when I was a kid. But when I grew up I realised that if I made my own book I could put anything I liked in it.

You could too.

You can draw any pictures or tell any story. You can make your story rhyme. Or not.

You can have big pictures and a few words. Or all words and no pictures. Or anything in-between. A story can be short too... just a few pages... or even one page or picture.

I've used paper, sticky-tape and scissors to make books by hand. But sometimes I have my books published so anyone can read them. This book is one of those.

Other books by Steve Attewell

Once, I Laughed My Socks Off

That's Twice I've Laughed My Socks Off

Printed in Great Britain
by Amazon